I love that you're my

Nana

because

I Love You Because Books
www.riverbreezepress.com

To Nana

Love, _____

Date: _____

The best thing about you is your

_____

Thank you for being patient with me when

_____

I remember when we

_____

You should win the grand prize for

_____

You make me feel special when

_____

Nana, I love you more than

_____

I love when you tell me about

_____

I love when we

_____

together

You taught me how to

_____

I know you love me because

_____

I wish I could

---

as well as
you do

Nana, I love that we have the same

_____

You should be the queen of

_____

You have an amazing talent for

_____

Nana, you make me laugh when you

_____

I wish I had more time to

_____

with you

You make the best

_____

You have inspired me to

_____

If I could give you anything it would be

_____

I would love to go

_____

with you

*You are
there for me when*

_____

Nana, I love you because you are

_____

Made in the USA
Las Vegas, NV
01 May 2024

89255135R00031